what am I?

A Picture Book of
Rhyming Winter Riddles

BY SHANA GORIAN

Written by Shana Gorian
Book Design by Four Fifty Six Design

First Edition, 2023

Take a ride downhill.

I go fast in the snow!

But pick up your feet,

or over, you'll go.

what am I?

A sled.

I dance in the air,
falling softly to the ground.
Like a crystal, I shimmer
and land gently on the ground.

what am I?

A snowflake.

I'm a drink that will warm you
from your head to your toes.
Chocolatey, delicious,
with tiny marshmallows.

what am I?

Hot cocoa.

I'm made up of snowballs,

big ones, at that.

You'll build me, then give me

a scarf and a hat.

what am I?

A snowman.

I'm a howling snowstorm
on a cold winter's night.
I make snow fall and wind blow
and block out the light.

what am I?

A blizzard.

I'm a piece of winter clothing, around your neck, you wear. I'll do my best to keep you warm and block the chilly air.

what am I?

A scarf.

If you want to keep
your feet from getting wet
out in the snow,
lace me up before
you leave the house.
Then off to play, you'll go!

What am I?

Boots.

If you want to twirl
across the ice,
then put your feet inside.
Lace me up and tie me tight,
then spin and whirl and glide.

What am I?

Ice skates.

Flap your arms and your legs
as you lay down in the snow.
What shape did you make?
I'll bet you know.

What am I?

A snow angel.

I'm something you wear on your feet in the snow to race down a mountain as fast as you'll go.

what am I?

skis.

I'm a card that you give
to express all your love
on a February holiday
that you must've heard of.

what am I?

A Valentine.

With my bow and my arrows
on Valentine's Day,
I spread love and friendship,
but I'm not real, they say.

What am I?

Cupid.

I'm a big strong bear
and my coat is white.
I live in the north,
but be careful—I bite!

what am I?

A polar bear.

I'm a black-and-white bird,
and I'm built for the cold.
I can swim but not fly,
and I'm cute, so I'm told.

what am I?

A penguin.

Shana Gorian is the author of the Rosco the Rascal series, early middle grade novels for kids ages 6-10. She loves holidays and seasons, and she loves to rhyme even when no one is listening.

Look for more seasonal, fun-loving books in the **What am I?** series for kids

Made in the USA
Middletown, DE
14 November 2024

64524075R00018